SWEDISH
TOYS, DOLLS AND GIFTS
YOU CAN MAKE YOURSELF

Välkommen! Welcome! That is how the friendly Swedish people would greet you if you came to their country. Sweden is a country famous for its beautiful handcrafts, as well as for its warm hospitality. Here is a colorful collection of easy-to-make dolls, toys, gifts, holiday foods and decorations in the Swedish style. Swedish artist, author and folklorist Ulf Löfgren shows and tells you just how you can make over 25 traditional handcraft objects. He has selected only projects that can be done by young children alone, or with a little help from an older child or adult, and using readily available materials.

A Dala horse, a jumping jack, Christmas elves and Easter witches, colorful wall hangings, a picturesque (and delicious!) gingerbread house, a hand puppet, a Viking ship model, and a lot of funny trolls are among the many attractive things you can make, following the clear and simple directions. And as you do, you'll also be getting to know something more about how Swedish children celebrate holidays, how they use the craft objects described, and some of the traditions behind them.

SWEDISH
TOYS, DOLLS AND GIFTS
YOU CAN MAKE YOURSELF

Traditional Swedish Handcrafts   By Ulf Löfgren

COLLINS + WORLD
New York and Cleveland
in cooperation with the U.S. Committee for UNICEF

A STORYCRAFT BOOK

Storycraft Books are specially designed to give young people an authentic introduction to the cultural traditions of other children around the world.

Special thanks are due to Ingalill Hjelm and Ronnie Krauss for their meticulous editing and assistance with the translation of the text, and their painstaking testing of the projects described in this book.

Library of Congress Cataloging in Publication data

Löfgren, Ulf.
Swedish toys, dolls, and gifts you can make yourself.
(A Storycraft book)
SUMMARY: Presents brief discussions of and easy-to-follow instructions for such traditional Swedish handicrafts as an Advent calendar, an Easter witch, and the Viking ship model.
    1. Handicraft—Sweden—Juvenile literature.
[1. Handicraft—Sweden.   2. Sweden—Social life and customs] I. Title. II. Series.
TT89.L63   745.5'09485   78-8619
         ISBN 0-529-05448-5   ISBN 0-529-05449-3 lib. bdg.

CONTENTS

ADVENT CALENDAR
Adventskalender

MATERIALS NEEDED: a piece of cloth (natural burlap is nice for this) 15 by 20 inches; a piece of red felt the same size; a coat hanger; needle and thread; a felt pen; scissors; paste; 24 small curtain rings; colored yarn; and 24 tiny gifts wrapped up in Christmas paper and tied with yarn.

Swedish children, like children all over the world, love Christmastime and can hardly wait to begin their holiday preparations. One way Swedish families mark December days is by making an Advent calendar like the one pictured here.

Fold the end of the cloth over the coat hanger and sew it across. Fringe the edges or hem them. With a felt pen draw a Santa Claus shape onto the felt and cut it out. Paste Santa to the cloth. Sew the 24 rings onto Santa's pouch, and tie the parcels to the rings with colored yarn. On the first of December, give the calendar to someone you love. Each day he or she can open one of the tiny gifts. That makes it easier to wait for Christmas to come!

SAFFRON BUNS
Saffransbröd

MATERIALS NEEDED: 1 envelope active dry yeast; ¼ cup warm water; large mixing bowl; 1 stick (¼ pound) butter; small saucepan; 1 cup light cream; ½ teaspoon salt; 2 eggs; ½ cup sugar; ½ teaspoon powdered saffron; 4 cups sifted all-purpose flour; baking sheet; raisins.

In Sweden it is a "must" to eat saffron bread at Christmas, and also on December 13, Saint Lucia's Day. At dawn, one of the children, dressed as Lucia, comes to wake the family, wearing a long white robe tied with a red sash, a crown of candles flickering on her head. She and her attendants carry a tray with coffee and saffron buns ...so good to eat!

Dissolve the yeast in the warm water in a large mixing bowl. Melt the butter in a small saucepan. Stir in the cream and then pour the lukewarm mixture into the yeast. Beat in the salt, one of the eggs, sugar, and saffron. Then gradually stir in the flour and work the dough until it is smooth. Cover and let it rise for half an hour.

Now turn the dough onto a lightly floured surface and knead it until it is smooth and shiny. Pinch off small pieces of dough and shape them into strips ½ inch wide and about 6 or 7 inches long. Shape these into any of the figures pictured here. Place the shaped rolls on a greased baking sheet and cover with a towel. Let rise until double in bulk, about 2 hours. Put a raisin in each S-shaped curl and brush with beaten egg. Bake in a preheated oven at 400°F. for 10 or 12 minutes. Makes 20 saffron buns.

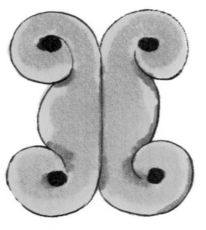

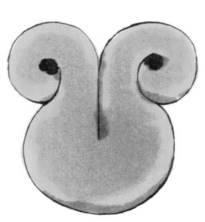

GINGERBREAD COOKIES
Pepparkakor

MATERIALS NEEDED: 3 sticks (¾ pound) of butter; 2 cups sugar; 1 cup dark corn syrup; 1½ tablespoons ginger; 1½ tablespoons cardamon; 1½ tablespoons cinnamon; 1 tablespoon cloves; 1½ cups whipping cream; 1 tablespoon baking soda; 9 cups sifted all-purpose flour; rolling pin; large nonstick-finish baking sheet; cookie cutters. (These ingredients will make dough for either gingerbread cookies or a gingerbread house; if you plan to make both, you must double each amount.)

Gingerbread takes some time to make, but it is fun to prepare and delicious to eat. It's best to make the dough the day before you plan to bake, so you can chill it overnight. This makes it easier to cut into shapes and also enhances the flavor of the spices.

Cream together the butter and sugar, then add the syrup and spices. Whip the cream until it starts to thicken and add. Mix the baking soda with half the flour and add to the batter. Gradually add the remaining flour. Turn the dough onto a lightly floured surface and knead until smooth. Put it in a plastic bag or return it to the bowl; cover it and put it in the refrigerator overnight.

Preheat the oven to 400°F. Roll out a small amount of the dough at a time on a large nonstick-finish baking sheet and cut it into shapes. If the dough sticks to the rolling pin, flour the rolling pin lightly. Roll the dough as thin as possible and cut it out with the cookie cutters into whatever shapes you like—hearts, stars, trees, etc. If you like, you can decorate them with blanched almonds. Bake them in the oven for 5 minutes, or until they are beautifully brown. Let the cookies cool before you remove them from the sheet. For some Helpful Hints, see page 31.

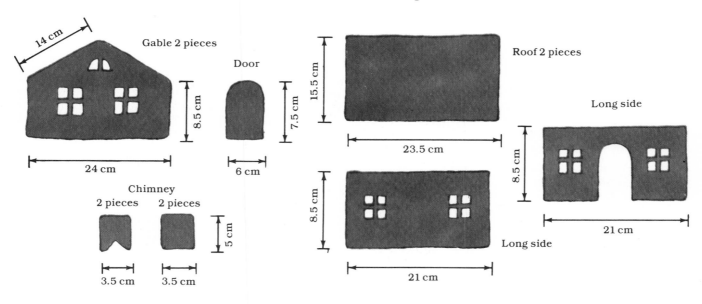

GINGERBREAD HOUSE

Pepparkakshus

MATERIALS NEEDED: same ingredients as for gingerbread cookies on page 10; wax paper; a frying pan; an egg beater; a sharp knife; 1 egg white; 2 cups confectioners' sugar; a pastry tube. For gluing the house together: 1 cup granulated sugar, 1 teaspoon white vinegar.

Use the same recipe to make the dough for the gingerbread house as for the gingerbread cookies. The pieces you cut out of the dough, however, will be the parts for the house. Roll the dough out on a clean nonstick baking sheet and cut out the sections in the sizes and shapes indicated on page 10. You can make patterns of wax paper and put them on the dough to guide you. Now cut along the edges with a knife. Cut out the windows and doors. Bake the pieces at 400°F. for about 15 minutes. Remove and trim the edges with a sharp knife. Let the pieces cool.

Now comes the fun of decorating. To make frosting, beat an egg white until stiff, then beat in 2 cups of confectioners' sugar. Put frosting into a pastry tube with a fine opening and squeeze out decorations of your own design. When the frosting has dried, melt 1 cup of granulated sugar and 1 teaspoon white vinegar in a frying pan over *very* low heat. When the sugar has turned light brown and liquid, dip into it those corners and edges of the house parts that you want to glue together and hold them pressed in place until they stick together. You must work very quickly, however, because the sugar "glue" will harden soon after it leaves the pan. Now decorate the roof with more frosting, and make some gingerbread trees and people to put around the house. You'd better watch out for nibblers, though, since gingerbread houses are everybody's favorite treat!

HEART BASKETS *Julgranskorgar*

MATERIALS NEEDED: colored paper; glue; scissors; a pencil compass.

Use a pencil compass to draw two circles 4 inches in diameter on different colored papers and cut them out. Fold both the circles in half. Holding one in each hand, put the right piece inside the left one. The folds should meet at the bottom, and flare out at the top to form a heart. Paste the inner half to the outer one, leaving the center open to fill with candy or nuts. Cut out a strip of paper, and paste an end to each side of the basket for a handle.

STARS *Julgranspynt*

MATERIALS NEEDED: toothpicks; modeling clay; thin string or heavy thread; gold or silver paper; scissors.

Roll modeling clay into balls the size of green peas. Stick toothpicks into the little balls and make squares or triangles. Let the clay dry. Hold the shapes together at opposite angles and tie with string where the bars cross. Cut stars or hearts out of gold or silver paper and make a tiny hole near the top of each. Thread with string and knot. Tie the other end of the string to a toothpick bar. Tie with string or heavy thread to the Christmas tree.

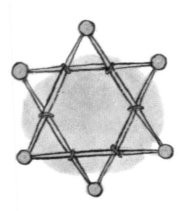

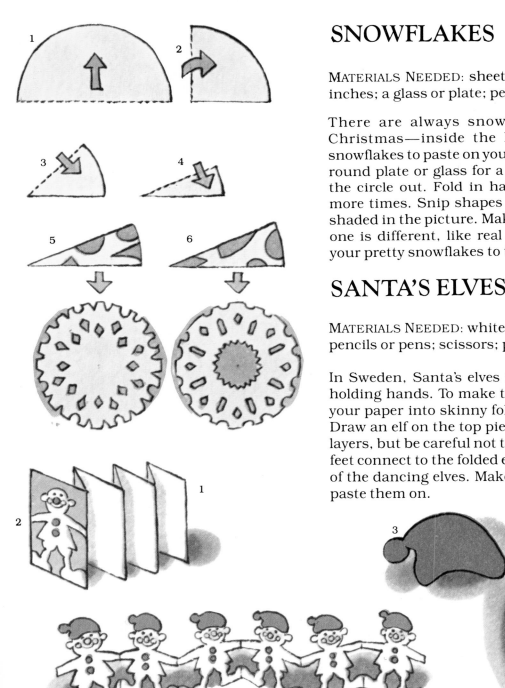

SNOWFLAKES *Snöflingor*

MATERIALS NEEDED: sheets of thin white paper 8 by 11 inches; a glass or plate; pencil; scissors; paste.

There are always snowflakes during the Swedish Christmas—inside the house as well as out! Make snowflakes to paste on your windows. Trace a circle (use a round plate or glass for a pattern) onto your paper. Cut the circle out. Fold in half once, then again, then two more times. Snip shapes out of the sides, like the ones shaded in the picture. Make up your own designs so each one is different, like real snowflakes. Unfold and paste your pretty snowflakes to the window.

SANTA'S ELVES *Tomtenissar*

MATERIALS NEEDED: white paper, 4 by 11 inches; colored pencils or pens; scissors; paste; red felt.

In Sweden, Santa's elves frolic on the Christmas table, holding hands. To make tomtenissar for your table, fold your paper into skinny folds like an accordian, as show. Draw an elf on the top piece. Cut the elf out through the layers, but be careful not to cut where the elf's hands and feet connect to the folded edge. Draw funny faces on each of the dancing elves. Make caps and suits of red felt and paste them on.

13

SANTA WITH SACK   *Tomte med tomtesäck*

MATERIALS NEEDED: two pieces of cardboard, 9 by 12 inches; a piece of red paper, the same size; transparent tape; a glass; scissors; colored pens; paste; small gifts already wrapped.

DIAGRAMS BELOW

Until Christmas Eve, Swedish children hide their gifts in a *tomtesäck* like the one that Santa Claus will use to carry the presents he brings on Christmas Eve.

Paste the red paper to one of the pieces of cardboard. Bend the cardboard around until the ends meet, and fasten together with tape. Trace around a glass to make a circle on the other piece of cardboard and cut the circle out. Draw two eyes, a nose, and a mouth on it, and paste it to the body. Also cut out arms, hands, buttons, a cap, and a beard from the cardboard and paste these onto the *tomte*. Hide small gifts, nicely wrapped, inside the sack. On the remaining cardboard, trace around the bottom of the tube-shaped sack. Cut out the cardboard circle and tape it firmly to the bottom of the tube so the presents will not fall out!

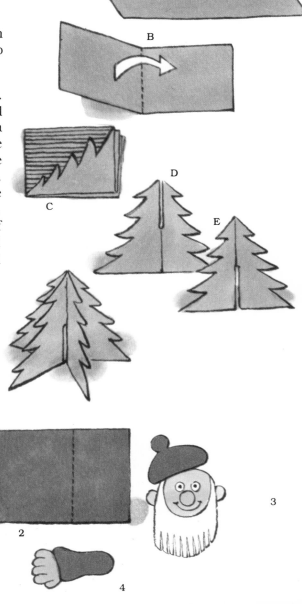

14

CHRISTMAS TREE *Julgran*

MATERIALS NEEDED: green construction or blotting paper, 9 by 12 inches; scissors.

DIAGRAMS ON OPPOSITE PAGE

Evergreens will add Christmas color to your windowsill or table. Fold the paper in half lengthwise (A). Now fold it in half the opposite way (B). Draw half a tree on the paper so that base of the tree is at the fold (C). Cut out the tree. You should now have two trees. Slit one tree halfway down from top to middle (D). Slit the other halfway up from bottom to middle (E). Fit them together to make a full three-dimensional standing tree.

CHRISTMAS ANGEL *Ängel*

MATERIALS NEEDED: a sheet of white paper, 9 by 12 inches; a pencil; a round plate; scissors; a quarter; paste; some gold paper; a toothpick; a styrofoam ball; straight pins; colored sequins; yellow and red yarn; a small glass.

DIAGRAMS AT RIGHT

(1) Trace round plate onto the white paper to make circle and cut it out. Trace a quarter in the very middle of the circle and cut it out, so there is a small hole in the center of the big circle. Make a cut from this hole to the circle's edge. Wrap the paper around to form a cone and paste or tape the overlapping pieces together. (2) Cut wings and hearts out of gold paper. Paste wings to the back and hearts to the front of the cone. (3) Stick a toothpick into a styrofoam ball and make an angel's face by sticking straight pins through sequins and then into the styrofoam for eyes, mouth, and nose. (4) Cut strips of yellow yarn for hair and tie at each end with red yarn. Glue to head. (5) Trace around the glass to make a circle on the gold paper, and cut it out. Paste to the back of the head as a halo. Put the head on the cone. The toothpick goes down inside to hold it in place. Now put your angel by your dinner place.

15

CHRISTMAS FIGURES
Juldekorationer

MATERIALS NEEDED: cardboard or thin plywood; paper and pencil; poster paints; scissors; a jigsaw if you use plywood; red ribbon.

At the beginning of Advent in Sweden it is a popular family tradition to hang a Star of Bethlehem with a candle (now usually an electric one) in the window. Then, just as dusk falls each December evening, all the stars are lighted, giving the streets a warm, friendly glow, so they look less lonely on the dark December nights.

As Christmas approaches, however, the windows begin to fill with other decorations like paper stars, snowflakes, angels, etc. Favorite window decorations are these "gingerbread" figures made of cardboard or plywood. Draw hearts and bells and other figures you like onto cardboard and cut them out with scissors; or trace shapes onto paper and transfer them to plywood; use the jigsaw to cut out wooden figures. Decorate with poster paints. Make a small hole near the top of each and hang with red ribbon in your window.

SNOWMAN *Snögubbe*

MATERIALS NEEDED: three 2-inch and six 1-inch styrofoam balls; two toothpicks; a pipe cleaner; yarn; a glass; a small round plate; cardboard; pencil; red felt; scissors; paste; sequins; pins; small buttons.

Snowy Swedish winters are perfect for building snowmen. Make this one at home. Trace the outline of the plate onto cardboard and cut out the circle to make a base. Glue three 2-inch styrofoam balls together and paste to the cardboard base. For each arm, glue together three 1-inch styrofoam balls. Attach to the body with the toothpicks. Use sequins to make eyes and a mouth on the head. Cut an inch off the pipe cleaner and stick it into the head for a nose. Use small buttons and attach with pins to the body. Cut a strip of felt 9 inches by 1 inch and tie around the neck for a scarf. Tie short strips of yarn to the pipe cleaner to make a broom. For a cap, trace the glass onto red felt and cut out the circle. Cut from the edge of the circle to the middle. Wrap the felt around until the ends slightly overlap. Paste the cap closed and put it on your snowman's head.

SKIING LAPP *Skidåkande Lapp*

MATERIALS NEEDED: one 2-inch and three 1-inch styrofoam balls; cardboard; ruler; pencils; scissors; white glue; a nickel; two toothpicks; two pipe cleaners; felt; sequins; pins; poster paints.

In northern Sweden, the Lapp people still breed reindeer. They love to ski across their snow-covered land. To make skis for the Lapp, cut two strips of cardboard 6 inches by 1 inch. Glue a 1-inch styrofoam ball to each. Glue both these legs to a 2-inch styrofoam-ball body. Glue a 1-inch ball on the top for a head. Trace two circles with the nickel onto cardboard and cut out the circle; stick a toothpick into each to make ski poles. Stick pipe cleaner arms into the Lapp's body and wrap each around a ski pole. Cut a piece of felt 4 by 1½ inches and paste pieces of yarn to the middle. Wrap it around the Lapp's head and paste it down. Use sequins to make a face. Paint a decorative coat onto the styrofoam.

EASTER TREE DECORATIONS
Påskris

MATERIALS NEEDED: 1-inch and 2-inch styrofoam balls; white glue or paste; several pieces of different colored felt, one of which is yellow; a safety pin; a 7-inch square of cloth; yarn; a small round plate; a felt pen; scissors; pipe cleaners.

During Lent, Swedish families gather birch branches, put them in a vase, and hang decorations on them. You can do the same with any kind of branches.

Here is the way to make a small Easter Witch to fly on your "tree." For her skirt, use a felt pen to trace the outline of the plate onto a piece of felt, and cut out the circle. Hold a 1-inch styrofoam ball in the center of the felt circle, and, from underneath, stick a safety pin through the felt into the ball, so that the pin lies flat and looks closed. Cut eyes, a mouth, and rosy cheeks out of felt and paste these onto the styrofoam head. Cut a triangle with 7-inch sides out of the cloth and tie it around the head for a scarf. Paste pieces of yarn to the forehead for hair. Make a broom by tying yarn strips to a 4-inch piece of pipe cleaner.

Puncture the witch's skirt with the scissors and set the broom into the hole. Stick a pipe cleaner into the top of her head; hook the other end onto a branch.

To make chicks to hang on the "tree," glue a 1-inch styrofoam ball to a 2-inch ball. Cut wings out of yellow felt and glue them to the body. Snip off an inch of pipe cleaner, bend it in half, and put it in the chick's head for a beak. Attach the chick to a branch with a pipe cleaner or thin wire.

Make a rooster by cutting out different colored pieces of felt. Glue together in the shape of a rooster, like the one pictured here. Puncture a hole in the top, thread with string, and tie the rooster to a branch.

EASTER EGGS
Påskägg

MATERIALS NEEDED: egg cartons; enamel paint; nontoxic watercolors; hardboiled eggs.

Since Easter comes in the Spring when hens begin to lay eggs again, it is customary in Sweden to give Easter presents of decorated cardboard eggs filled with candy. To make these yourself, break egg cartons into their individual "pockets." Usually each pocket is the shape of half an egg. Decorate two halves with enamel paint and fill them with jelly beans. Tape them together and give them to someone you like a lot!

Families also have "egg feasts" at Easter. Gather everyone (and invite your friends, too) around the kitchen table and paint hard-boiled eggs with nontoxic watercolors. See who can make the prettiest eggs—and then feast on them!

EASTER WITCH
Påskkäring

MATERIALS NEEDED: a piece of cardboard 12 inches square; a pencil; a round plate; scissors; a quarter; a 12-inch square of black felt; paste; a 2-inch styrofoam ball; a toothpick; yarn; a 10-inch square of cloth; pipe cleaners; felt scraps.

It is an old Swedish belief that witches flew to Blåkulla to celebrate Easter, carrying black cats and copper kettles on their broomsticks. On Easter Eve, Swedish girls and boys dress up as witches and bring Easter greetings to their neighbors. Here's a witch on her way to Blåkulla, now!

Trace the outline of a round plate onto the cardboard and cut out the circle. Trace the outline of the quarter in the middle of the circle. Cut from the circle's edge to the center, and cut out the circle so that there is a hole left in the center. Now repeat these directions using the black felt, instead of the cardboard. Paste the felt to the cardboard, and when the paste has dried, wrap it around to form a cone. Paste it closed. Cut out felt eyes, mouth, cheeks, and nose, and paste them to the styrofoam ball. Stick a toothpick into the ball, and drop it into the cone so that the head sits on the cardboard dress. Paste yarn on her forehead. Cut out a triangle with 10-inch sides from the piece of cloth. Tie it around her head. With scissors, puncture the cardboard dress in the front and in the back. Make a broom by tying yarn strips to the end of a pipe cleaner. Pass the broom through the dress holes. Using the cat and kettle you see here as a pattern, draw and cut them out from cardboard. Trace the cat onto black felt and the kettle onto yellow. Paste the felt to the matching cardboard shapes. Hang the kettle from the broomstick and let the cat sit behind the witch.

Model for shawl

Model for body

EASTER ROOSTER
(Egg Warmer and Wall Decoration)
Påsktupp

Egg Warmer

MATERIALS NEEDED: two felt squares, 5 by 5 inches; different colored pieces of felt; pencil and paper; scissors; needle and thread.

Make an egg warmer for your Easter morning eggs or for Easter gifts. Trace outline of the rooster in the picture onto paper and cut the paper rooster out to use as a pattern. Pin the 2 squares together and cut your bird out of both squares at the same time. Draw and cut out of different colored felt the comb, tail, and wattle. Place these pieces, except the tail, in between the two body pieces and then stitch together where you see the dotted line on the picture. Paste the tail feathers to the back. Now slip the rooster over your egg to keep it warm!

Rooster Wall Hanging

MATERIALS NEEDED: heavy cardboard or thin wood (the size board will depend on the size picture you want); a piece of cloth the same size; scissors; different colored pieces of felt; paste; wire.

Put this colorful rooster on your wall! Paste cloth to the cardboard or wood. Cut out different colored pieces of felt and paste them together on the cloth to make a rooster like the one pictured below. You can trace this rooster and enlarge with the grid (see page 31 for instructions) if you like. Puncture holes in the cardboard (or ask an older friend to drill holes if you use wood) and hang with wire.

JUMPING JACK *Sprattelgubbe*

MATERIALS NEEDED: a piece of heavy cardboard, 12 by 12 inches; colored pens; craft knife or strong scissors; a paper punch; 8 paper clips; fasteners; string.

Jumping Jacks have always been favorite Swedish toys. This one is wearing the traditional Swedish folk costume, which you can copy. Enlarge the sections of Jack's figure from those shown below at the left and draw them onto the cardboard. (See page 31 to learn how to enlarge a drawing.) Cut out the parts. Use the paper punch to make holes as shown. Fasten the arm pieces together at the elbows with paper fasteners. Fasten the legs together at the knees. Fasten the arms and legs to the body using the *second* hole from the top of the upper arms and thighs. Cut four short pieces of string and thread one through each remaining hole in the upper arms and thighs. Tie all to a center string that extends down the back (see picture). Knot the string at the end, and, when you pull on it, your Jack will jump!

HAND PUPPET *Handmarionett*

MATERIALS NEEDED: a small round bottle or jar that your middle finger fits into (a small tube-shaped plastic pill-bottle is good for this); 5 or 6 newspaper pages shredded into strips; 1 cup flour; 1 cup of water (approximately); 2 felt squares 12 inches by 12 inches; a felt square about 5 inches by 5 inches, of another color; paste; enamel or poster paints; yellow yarn; a triangle of brightly colored material; needle and thread.

Here is a hand puppet dressed in a Swedish folk costume. To make this puppet, first make *papier mâché*. Mix flour and water into a thick paste. Cut newspapers into strips about an inch wide and soak some of them in the paste. This makes a very good, sticky sort of "clay" from which you can model your puppet's head and neck. Turn the jar upside down; build the puppet's head and a short neck around the base of the jar with the papier mâché, and let it dry. (This might take overnight.) Paint it flesh color and let the paint dry; then add a mouth, cheeks, eyes and nose with the other colors. Cut strips of yarn and paste them to the head for hair. Tie a triangle of brightly colored or decorated material around her head for a kerchief. Using the pattern in the picture for the puppet's dress, enlarge it to a size (see page 31 for instructions) that will fit around your hand and then trace it onto the 2 felt squares. Cut out both at once, and sew up the sides, leaving a hole at the neck (and at the bottom, of course). Attach dress to the head and neck of the puppet by wrapping a rubber band, thread or a twist-tie tightly around the neckline. Now put the puppet over your hand. Your index finger goes inside the head; your thumb and middle finger move the arms. Fold your other two fingers under. Raise the curtain and begin the play!

NILS HOLGERSSON *Nils Holgersson*

MATERIALS NEEDED: tracing paper; pencil; cardboard; scissors; green felt; paste.

One of Sweden's best-loved books is *The Adventures of Nils Holgersson*, by Selma Lagerlöf. It is the story of Nils Holgersson, a little boy who flew over Sweden on the back of a goose. To create your own set for Nils's story, begin with a scene of Nils at home. Trace the patterns of Nils and his goose, and use the grid to make them the size you want. Transfer them onto cardboard, and cut them out. Fold on the indicated dotted lines to stand them up. Trace and use the grid to make the tree and cottage, too, but put these onto cardboard which you have doubled over. When you cut out the trees and house, do *not* cut where the cardboard is folded over, and they will stand up on their own. Place all pieces on a cardboard base. You can even paste down green felt "grass" on the base.

ANIMALS OF SKANSEN
Djuren på Skansen

MATERIALS NEEDED: several sheets of white cardboard; colored pens; scissors; a small round plate; green felt; white glue or paste.

In Stockholm, the capital of Sweden, there is a famous park called Skansen. At the zoo there, you can see all the different kinds of animals to be found in Sweden. Make your own Skansen zoo by drawing animals onto the cardboard with an extra flap of cardboard drawn under the feet to be folded back and used as a base for them to stand on. Cut the animals out and bend the base back. Trace the outline of the small plate onto cardboard and cut the circle out; paste green felt "grass" down on it and glue the animal's base to it. Cut out thin cardboard strips about 1 inch wide for a fence, and glue or paste the pieces together to enclose the circle of grass. Decorate the fence and, if you like, make trees, too, for the animals to sleep under.

25

TROLLS *Troll*

Troll Hanger

MATERIALS NEEDED: two pieces of heavy cardboard, 12 by 24 inches; a coat hanger; enamel or poster paints.

Perhaps you have heard of the mischievous trolls which, it's said, live in the forests of Sweden. They are funny-looking creatures with big warty noses and long tails. Some are good-natured and some are mean, but when you make your own, they are always fun to have around.

To make a troll clothes hanger, trace a hanger shape onto heavy cardboard and cut it out. Two thicknesses of cardboard glued together make a sturdier hanger. Paint the funniest, ugliest face you can think of on it. Be sure to let the paint dry before you hang your clothes on it!

Troll Sculptures

MATERIALS NEEDED: rocks of all sizes; strong glue; enamel paints; wire or pipe cleaners; yarn.

Make a troll sculpture from rocks you find outside at the beach or in the yard. Use a big one for the body and little ones for the head, nose,

arms, feet. Glue them together and paint an ugly face on the head with enamel paint. Glue yarn on the head for hair. Braid some yarn on a piece of thin wire or pipe cleaner for a curving tail. Fasten the tail by wedging one end into a crevice between the rocks. Watch out that the troll doesn't smack you with his tail!

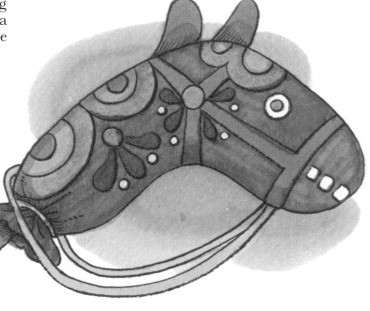

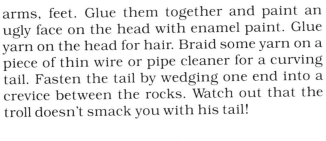

HOBBYHORSE *Käpphäst*

MATERIALS NEEDED: an old sock (a big knitted ski sock is best); filler material (this can be old scraps of cloth or foam rubber); needle and thread; a broomstick; different colored pieces of felt; paste; string or ribbon.

Ride a hobbyhorse from Dalarna to Stockholm and home again.

Stuff an old sock with filler material and stick a broomstick securely into it. Sew or tie together tightly at the open end. Cut eyes, teeth, bridle, and decorative markings from felt and paste them onto the sock. Cut out ears of felt and sew onto the head. Make reins from string or ribbon to guide your horse.

VIKING SHIP
Vikingaskepp

MATERIALS NEEDED: a large sheet of cardboard; a piece of white construction paper; white glue or paste; scissors; a craft knife; tape; a round plate about 6 inches in diameter; poster paints; colored markers.

1. Using the plate, which should measure about 6 inches in diameter, draw two half circles on the cardboard, forming an ellipse that measures about 2 inches at the widest point.

2. Draw a rectangle, about 4 by 5½ inches, around the ellipse leaving 1 inch on either side, as shown, and cut out the rectangle, using your scissors.

3. Then, with the craft knife, carefully cut along the curved lines, without cutting all the way through the cardboard. This is called "scoring" the cardboard.

4. You can, then, bend the cardboard to make the shape of the boat by pulling together the shorter ends of the rectangle and taping them. Paint the boat a bright color.

5. Cut out a small V-shaped angle in the boat, as shown. Make a mast by cutting a 7- by ½-inch strip of cardboard. Score the cardboard, as you did the curved lines of the boat, down the center of the mast. Fold along the scored line and insert the mast into the V-shaped cut you made. Secure the mast to the boat with a drop of glue or paste.

6. Cut a 4- by 5-inch piece of white construction paper for a sail. Paint red stripes, as shown. Make two small holes, ½ inch from the top and ½ inch from the bottom, slide the sail onto the mast, and secure with a drop of glue at either end.

7. Make a dragon figurehead by cutting a 4½-inch strip of cardboard in the shape shown

7

8

here. Draw in eyes, nostrils, and teeth, and paint or color the dragon brightly. Score the upper side of the head along the dotted line, as shown. Score the underside of the dragon down the middle from the head to the end. Fold along the scored lines and secure the figurehead to the front of the ship with glue, as shown in the picture.

8. Decorate your Viking ship with shields cut from cardboard and a streamer cut from construction paper, painted in bright colors, and glued in place on the ship, as shown.

ARCHIPELAGO STEAMSHIP *Skärgårdsbåtar*

MATERIALS NEEDED: blocks of wood; small cardboard boxes and tubes; hammer and small nails; sharp knife; scissors; glue, thread; poster paints; imagination.

In the archipelago, or group of small islands in the Baltic Sea around Sweden's capital city of Stockholm, there is a beautiful sight. Some very old but well-preserved white steamships still sail to and fro among the lush green islands, ferrying passengers in elegant style. To build your own Archipelago Steamship, begin with a suitably-shaped block of wood for the hull. You can nail on an upper cabin of wood or glue on one made of cardboard. Paint boat white. Follow the Viking ship directions to make the mast

and glue to the lower deck. The funnel, which you can make by painting a toilet paper cardboard tube, should be glued or taped to the top deck. Use your imagination to make and attach rails, lifeboats and any other accessories a steamship might need for sailing the Stockholm Archipelago.

DALA HORSE *Dalahäst*

MATERIALS NEEDED: 2 pieces of cardboard or thin wood, 12 by 12 inches; a piece of natural burlap to cover the cardboard (cloth or felt will also work); a piece of red felt, 12 by 12 inches; different colored pieces of felt; colored masking tape 1¼ inches wide; paper and pencil; poster paints; a felt pen; a craft knife or scissors; paste; wire; a jigsaw, if you decide to make a wooden horse.

If you go to Sweden you will see that the favorite souvenir to bring home is a Dala Horse, made in the province of Dalarna. To make your own, either trace the horse pictured here and enlarge with the grid (page 31) or draw your own to the size you want. In Sweden a Dala Horse is carved out of wood with a jigsaw, as shown, and you can make one this way, or you can cut one out of heavy cardboard with a craft knife or scissors. Paint the horse red with poster paints and decorate it in bright colors. You can hang it on your wall as is, or glue it into the frame as described below. Or, instead of wood, you can make your horse of felt. Trace your horse-shape onto red felt and cut it out. Cut out different colored felt pieces and decorate it beautifully. To make a frame for your Dala Horse, cover a square piece of wood or cardboard with natural burlap and paste the burlap down. Fold and paste the borders neatly over the edges all around it. Put colored masking tape around all sides to border the burlap. Paste the red felt horse directly onto the burlap in the frame. Make two small holes near the top of the frame and string fine wires through them so you can hang your Dala Horse proudly on your wall.

HELPFUL HINTS

Enlarging Patterns and Drawings

To enlarge a drawing or pattern such as the jumping jack on page 22, trace the drawing onto a piece of plain paper and with a ruler and pencil draw a "grid" pattern of evenly sized squares on top of it. If you want your new pattern to be three times as big, draw a new grid on a large piece of paper, with the same number of squares, making each square three times as big as the squares on the smaller grid. Now, starting with the square in the upper left hand corner, copy the lines in each square of the small grid onto the corresponding square in the larger grid. Do this with each square. You will be surprised how well you can do this. When you have finished, check your drawing against the original one, and make any small corrections you may need to make it look just right. You can enlarge any drawing or pattern this way.

Gingerbread Baking Hints

If the dough still has bubbles when you have taken it out of the refrigerator and are ready to use it, roll it first on a *cold* plate. Then roll it out on the large nonstick baking sheet and cut it into shapes, trimming away the extra dough and leaving just the shape you want. (*Don't* cut your cookies on a separate board and then try to move them onto the baking sheet!) Put a damp cloth or teatowel between your table top and the baking sheet so it won't slip when you are rolling the dough. If the dough becomes too soft and smeary, pop the whole baking sheet into the refrigerator for 15 minutes and then continue rolling. You can use the excess dough trimmed away from the cookies. Chill it, roll it out again, and cut into more cookie shapes.

THINKING METRIC

The measurements in this book have been given in Metric System units. To change centimeters into inches, multiply by .3937. For example, the gingerbread house is 21 centimeters long; $21 \times .3937 = 8.2677$, or about eight and one-quarter inches. There are 2.54 centimeters in one inch.

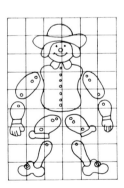

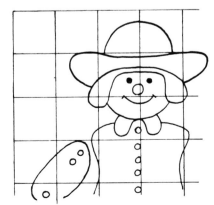

About Ulf Löfgren

Ulf Löfgren's interest in folklore and crafts is of long standing. A graduate of Uppsala University, his fields of study were history of art and history of literature and folklore. He began to illustrate picture books in 1959 after several years of pursuing a career in advertising, and his very first book brought him the Elsa Beskow Award, a greatly acclaimed honor in Sweden. Since then he has won plaques at the Bratislava International Biennale in 1971, 1973, and 1975; and in 1977 he won the Grand Prix there. He has been the chairman of the Swedish Society of Illustrators (1971-1975) and his work is exhibited in the Swedish National Gallery. He also creates television shows for children and has made at least a hundred programs for Swedish Television to date.

He lives with his wife, who is a teacher, and their two children in Lidingö, a small town near Stockholm. In the summertime they vacation on an island in the Baltic Sea where they own a big old house that creaks and groans with age, and keeps them very busy. Besides protecting the house against the ravages of time, Mr. Löfgren's other main hobby is playing the violin.

J
745.5
L
 Lofgren, Ulf
 Swedish toys, dolls, and gifts you
can make yourself...